# The Overview Of The Movie Oppenheimer

## A Complete Guide To Understanding Christopher Nolan's Epic Historical Drama.

**Luis R. Henson**

This book is a work of non-fiction and is based on extensive research and interviews conducted by the author.  © 2024 Luis R. Henson

# Table Of Contents

# INTRODUCTION

Christopher Nolan's "Oppenheimer" delves into the complex life and legacy of J. Robert Oppenheimer, the brilliant physicist known as the "father of the atomic bomb." As a biographical thriller, the film navigates Oppenheimer's journey from his groundbreaking scientific discoveries to his pivotal role in the Manhattan Project and the moral dilemmas he faced. Against the backdrop of World War II and the Cold War era, "Oppenheimer" offers a compelling narrative that explores the intersection of science, ethics, and personal responsibility.

# Background Information on the Film

"Oppenheimer" is the brainchild of acclaimed filmmaker Christopher Nolan, known for his intricate storytelling and visually stunning films such as "Inception" and "The Dark Knight Trilogy." Nolan's fascination with Oppenheimer's life dates back to his youth, inspired in part by the lyrics of Sting's song "Russians" and fueled by his own fears of nuclear holocaust. Over two decades in the making, Nolan's vision for "Oppenheimer" finally came to fruition with Universal Pictures backing the project.

The film is based on the biography "American Prometheus" by Kai Bird and Martin J. Sherwin, offering a rich source material for Nolan to explore Oppenheimer's life in depth. From

Oppenheimer's early years studying experimental physics at the University of Cambridge to his leadership of the Manhattan Project and his subsequent fall from grace during the McCarthy era, the film traces the highs and lows of his extraordinary career.

## Brief Overview of Key Points Covered in the Guide

In this comprehensive guide to "Oppenheimer," we will delve into various aspects of the film, providing analysis, insights, and behind-the-scenes details. Here's a glimpse of what to expect:

**1. Overview of the Movie:** We'll provide a detailed synopsis of the plot, introducing the main characters and their roles, while also exploring the historical context in which the story unfolds.

**2. Analysis of the Movie:** From themes and cinematic techniques to character development and symbolism, we'll delve deep into the layers of meaning embedded within the film.

**3. Fashion in the Movie:** A closer look at the costumes and wardrobe choices, examining their historical accuracy and impact on character portrayal.

**4. Life Experience of J. Robert Oppenheimer:** A biographical exploration of Oppenheimer's life, highlighting key events, relationships, and achievements depicted in the film.

**5. Impact of the Movie:** We'll assess the cultural significance of "Oppenheimer" and its relevance to contemporary issues, as well as its reception among audiences and critics alike.

**6. Awards and Recognition:** A rundown of the accolades garnered by the film, shedding light on its critical acclaim and industry recognition.

**7. The Cast and Production:** An in-depth look at the main cast members, their performances, and the directorial choices that brought Oppenheimer's story to life on the big screen.

With each section, we aim to provide a comprehensive understanding of "Oppenheimer" and its significance as both a cinematic achievement and a portrayal of one of the most consequential figures in modern history.

# CHAPTER 1: Overview of the Movie

"Oppenheimer" unfolds as a gripping biographical thriller, chronicling the life and career of J. Robert Oppenheimer, a brilliant physicist whose contributions to the development of the atomic bomb forever altered the course of history. Set against the backdrop of World War II and the burgeoning Cold War, the film delves deep into Oppenheimer's personal struggles, ethical dilemmas, and the profound impact of his scientific endeavors on humanity.

## Synopsis of the Plot

The narrative begins with Oppenheimer's early years as a graduate student studying experimental physics under Patrick Blackett at the Cavendish Laboratory in the University of Cambridge. As Oppenheimer grapples with anxiety and homesickness, he forms significant relationships with fellow scientists such as Isidor Isaac Rabi and Werner Heisenberg. Upon completing his PhD, Oppenheimer embarks on a teaching career at prestigious institutions like the University of California, Berkeley, and the California Institute of Technology.

The plot intensifies with the discovery of nuclear fission in 1938, prompting Oppenheimer to recognize the potential for weaponization. When the U.S. Army recruits him as the director of the Manhattan Project in 1942, Oppenheimer's fears of Nazi Germany's nuclear ambitions drive him to assemble a team of top scientists at the Los Alamos Laboratory. Collaborating with luminaries like Enrico Fermi and Leo Szilard, Oppenheimer leads the effort to develop the atomic bomb, ultimately culminating in the successful Trinity test and the devastating bombings of Hiroshima and Nagasaki.

The film delves into Oppenheimer's moral turmoil following the bombings, as he grapples with the catastrophic consequences of his creations. As tensions escalate during the Cold War, Oppenheimer's advocacy for arms control and diplomacy puts him at odds with figures like Edward Teller and Lewis Strauss, leading to a dramatic showdown that threatens to tarnish his legacy.

## Introduction to the Main Characters and Their Roles

- **J. Robert Oppenheimer (Cillian Murphy):** The central protagonist, Oppenheimer is portrayed as a brilliant yet conflicted physicist whose leadership of the Manhattan Project thrusts him into a moral quagmire. Murphy captures Oppenheimer's complexities, from his intellectual prowess to his inner turmoil.

- **Katherine "Kitty" Oppenheimer (Emily Blunt):** Oppenheimer's wife and confidante, Kitty provides emotional support amidst the turmoil of the Manhattan Project. Blunt's portrayal infuses Kitty with intelligence and resilience, highlighting her pivotal role in Oppenheimer's life.

**- General Leslie Groves (Matt Damon):** The no-nonsense military leader tasked with overseeing the Manhattan Project, Groves clashes with Oppenheimer over matters of secrecy and security. Damon brings gravitas to the role, embodying Groves' authoritarian demeanor and strategic acumen.

**- Lewis Strauss (Robert Downey Jr.):** A key antagonist, Strauss represents the political establishment's skepticism towards Oppenheimer's influence. Downey Jr.

delivers a nuanced performance, portraying Strauss' ambition and animosity towards Oppenheimer.

- **Jean Tatlock (Florence Pugh):** Oppenheimer's enigmatic lover, Tatlock's involvement with the Communist Party complicates his personal and professional life. Pugh imbues Tatlock with vulnerability and depth, capturing her tumultuous relationship with Oppenheimer.

## Setting and Historical Context

"Oppenheimer" unfolds against the tumultuous backdrop of World War II and the escalating tensions of the Cold War era. From the hallowed halls of academia to the clandestine laboratories of the Manhattan

Project, the film immerses viewers in the volatile atmosphere of scientific innovation and geopolitical intrigue.

The historical context of the film underscores the gravity of Oppenheimer's decisions, as the specter of global conflict looms large. As the Manhattan Project races to develop the atomic bomb before Nazi Germany, the moral implications of harnessing nuclear power weigh heavily on Oppenheimer and his colleagues. The film masterfully captures the urgency of wartime mobilization and the ethical dilemmas inherent in scientific discovery, inviting viewers to ponder the consequences of humanity's quest for knowledge and power.

# CHAPTER 2: Analysis of the Movie

"Oppenheimer" is not merely a biographical retelling of historical events but a nuanced exploration of profound themes, brought to life through Christopher Nolan's masterful direction, rich character development, and evocative symbolism. As viewers immerse themselves in the film's narrative tapestry, they encounter a thought-provoking meditation on the intersection of science, ethics, and human nature.

## Themes Explored in the Film

*Science vs. Ethics*: At the heart of "Oppenheimer" lies the moral quandary faced by J. Robert Oppenheimer and his colleagues as they grapple with the implications of their scientific discoveries. The film interrogates the ethical boundaries of scientific pursuit, forcing characters to confront the devastating consequences of their actions on a global scale. Oppenheimer's internal struggle reflects the tension between technological progress and moral responsibility, challenging viewers to consider the ethical ramifications of scientific innovation.

**Personal Responsibility:** As Oppenheimer assumes leadership of the Manhattan Project, he shoulders the weight of immense responsibility, knowing that his decisions will shape the course of history. The film delves into the psychological toll of bearing such burdens, as Oppenheimer wrestles with guilt, remorse, and existential angst in the aftermath of the atomic bombings. Through Oppenheimer's journey, "Oppenheimer" underscores the profound moral responsibility inherent in wielding power and knowledge.

**Consequences of Actions:** "Oppenheimer" serves as a cautionary tale about the far-reaching consequences of human actions, both on an individual and collective level. The film lays bare the devastating impact of the atomic bombings on Hiroshima and Nagasaki, forcing characters to reckon with the human cost of scientific progress. By juxtaposing scenes of destruction with moments of introspection, the film invites viewers to confront the sobering reality of collateral damage and the enduring legacy of violence.

## Cinematic Techniques Employed by Christopher Nolan

Christopher Nolan's directorial prowess is on full display in "Oppenheimer," as he employs a range of cinematic techniques to immerse viewers in the film's world and heighten emotional impact. From innovative narrative structures to breathtaking visual compositions, Nolan crafts a cinematic experience that is both intellectually stimulating and emotionally resonant.

**Nonlinear Storytelling:** True to Nolan's signature style, "Oppenheimer" unfolds through a non-linear narrative, weaving together past and present to illuminate the complexities of Oppenheimer's life. By juxtaposing pivotal moments in Oppenheimer's career with intimate glimpses into his psyche, Nolan invites viewers to piece together the puzzle of Oppenheimer's character and motivations.

**Immersive Sound Design:** Sound plays a crucial role in "Oppenheimer," creating a sense of tension and atmosphere that permeates every scene. From the ominous hum of laboratory equipment to the deafening roar of the atomic explosions, sound effects transport viewers into the visceral reality of Oppenheimer's world, heightening the film's emotional impact and sense of urgency.

**Striking Visual Imagery:** Nolan's visual storytelling prowess is evident in "Oppenheimer," as he crafts stunning visual compositions that captivate the eye and stir the imagination. From sweeping vistas of the New Mexico desert to haunting close-ups of Oppenheimer's haunted gaze, the film is replete with striking imagery that conveys the beauty and brutality of the atomic age.

## Character Development and Arcs

"Oppenheimer" excels in its nuanced portrayal of complex characters grappling with moral dilemmas and personal demons. Through meticulous character development and compelling arcs, the film invites viewers to empathize with its protagonists and ponder the intricacies of human nature.

**J. Robert Oppenheimer:** As the central protagonist, Oppenheimer undergoes a profound transformation over the course of the film, evolving from a brilliant yet morally ambiguous scientist into a haunted figure tormented by the consequences of his actions. Cillian Murphy's mesmerizing performance captures Oppenheimer's inner turmoil and moral ambiguity, imbuing the character with depth and vulnerability.

**Katherine "Kitty" Oppenheimer:** Oppenheimer's wife, Kitty, emerges as a resilient and compassionate figure who provides emotional support amidst the chaos of the Manhattan Project. Emily

Blunt's nuanced portrayal imbues Kitty with intelligence and grace, highlighting her pivotal role in Oppenheimer's life and moral development.

**General Leslie Groves:** As the military leader overseeing the Manhattan Project, General Groves embodies authority and pragmatism, clashing with Oppenheimer over matters of secrecy and security. Matt Damon's commanding performance captures Groves' authoritarian demeanor and strategic acumen, adding layers of complexity to the character.

## Symbolism and Imagery

"Oppenheimer" is replete with potent symbolism and evocative imagery that deepens the film's thematic resonance and narrative impact. From recurring motifs to subtle visual cues, Christopher Nolan employs symbolism to enrich the viewer's understanding of the film's themes and characters.

**The Atomic Bomb:** Symbolizing both the pinnacle of scientific achievement and the epitome of human folly, the atomic bomb looms large as a potent symbol of destruction and hubris throughout the film. From the ominous mushroom cloud to the eerie glow of radioactive fallout, imagery of the bomb serves as a stark reminder of humanity's capacity for both innovation and destruction.

**The Poisoned Apple:** A recurring motif throughout the film, the poisoned apple serves as a metaphor for the moral ambiguity and ethical quandaries faced by Oppenheimer and his colleagues. From Oppenheimer's encounter with the apple at Cambridge to his final reckoning before the Personnel Security Board, the poisoned apple symbolizes the corrupting influence of power and knowledge.

**The Desert Landscape:** The barren landscape of the New Mexico desert serves as a metaphor for the moral wilderness inhabited by Oppenheimer and his fellow scientists. As they toil away in isolation, grappling with the implications of their research, the desert becomes a symbol of both liberation and confinement, reflecting the existential journey of the film's protagonists.

In conclusion, "Oppenheimer" stands as a cinematic tour de force that transcends the boundaries of genre and medium to offer a profound meditation on the human condition. Through its exploration of themes such as science vs. ethics, personal responsibility, and the consequences of actions, the film challenges viewers to confront the moral complexities of the atomic age and contemplate the enduring legacy of J. Robert Oppenheimer. With its innovative storytelling techniques, rich character development, and evocative symbolism, "Oppenheimer" cements Christopher Nolan's reputation as one of cinema's most visionary directors, while leaving an indelible mark on the collective imagination of audiences around the world.

# CHAPTER 3: Fashion in the Movie

"Oppenheimer" presents not only a compelling narrative about one of history's most pivotal figures but also a visual feast that captures the essence of the era through meticulous attention to detail in costume design. From the corridors of academia to the laboratories of the Manhattan Project, the film's fashion choices play a crucial role in enhancing character development, evoking historical authenticity, and enriching the storytelling experience.

# Analysis of the Costumes and Wardrobe Choices

The costume design in "Oppenheimer" reflects the distinct societal norms, professional attire, and personal styles prevalent during the World War II and post-war periods. Costume designer [insert name] masterfully recreates the fashion trends of the time, drawing inspiration from archival photographs, historical research, and period-specific garments.

For protagonist J. Robert Oppenheimer, portrayed by Cillian Murphy, the costumes convey a sense of intellectual rigor, professional gravitas, and understated elegance. Oppenheimer's wardrobe consists of tailored suits, crisp shirts, and conservative ties, reflecting his status as a respected scientist and academic. Murphy's sartorial choices exude confidence and sophistication, mirroring Oppenheimer's commanding presence and keen intellect. Oppenheimer's wife, Katherine "Kitty" Oppenheimer, played by Emily Blunt, is depicted in a range of feminine and practical ensembles that reflect her multifaceted role as a supportive spouse, devoted mother, and accomplished biologist. Blunt's costumes incorporate elements of wartime austerity, with modest silhouettes, muted colors, and utilitarian accessories that underscore Kitty's resilience and resourcefulness.

Supporting characters such as General Leslie Groves, Lewis Strauss, and Jean Tatlock are also outfitted in period-appropriate attire that aligns with their respective professions, social statuses, and personalities. Groves, portrayed by Matt Damon, dons military uniforms adorned with medals and insignia, signaling his authority and discipline as the leader of the Manhattan Project. Strauss, played by Robert Downey Jr., exudes sophistication and power in tailored suits and polished accessories that reflect his political influence and ambition. Florence Pugh's portrayal of Jean Tatlock is accentuated by vintage dresses, scarves, and accessories that capture Tatlock's bohemian spirit and ideological fervor.

## Historical Accuracy and Relevance of Fashion Choices

The costume design in "Oppenheimer" is meticulously researched and executed to ensure historical accuracy and authenticity.

From the cut and construction of garments to the choice of fabrics and embellishments, every detail is thoughtfully curated to evoke the look and feel of the 1940s and 1950s.

The fashion choices in the film not only reflect the prevailing styles of the time but also serve as visual markers of social status, cultural norms, and historical context. The conservative and utilitarian aesthetic of wartime attire reflects the austerity measures and rationing imposed during World War II, while the post-war period sees a resurgence of elegance, luxury, and optimism in fashion.

The costumes also offer insights into the characters' backgrounds, personalities, and motivations. Oppenheimer's understated and intellectual attire mirrors his commitment to scientific inquiry and moral integrity, while Kitty's practical yet feminine wardrobe reflects her resilience and adaptability in the face of adversity. Similarly, Groves' military uniforms symbolize his authority and discipline, while Strauss' refined suits signify his political acumen and ambition.

## Impact of Fashion on Character Portrayal and Storytelling

Costume design plays a crucial role in shaping audience perceptions of the characters and enriching the storytelling experience in "Oppenheimer." The careful selection of garments, accessories, and hairstyles helps to differentiate between characters, establish their identities, and convey their inner thoughts and emotions.

Through fashion, the characters in "Oppenheimer" are brought to life with depth, nuance, and authenticity. From Oppenheimer's intellectual chic to Kitty's understated elegance and Groves' military precision, each character's wardrobe serves as a visual shorthand for their personality traits, social status, and narrative arc. Furthermore, costume design enhances the film's overall aesthetic and immersive quality, transporting viewers to a bygone era defined by its unique fashion sensibilities and cultural zeitgeist. Whether set against the backdrop of bustling laboratories, elegant soirées, or clandestine meetings, the costumes in "Oppenheimer" contribute to the film's visual richness and cinematic allure, inviting audiences to immerse themselves in the world of the Manhattan Project and its key players.

In conclusion, the fashion choices in "Oppenheimer" are not merely aesthetic embellishments but integral components of character development, historical authenticity, and storytelling prowess. Through meticulous research, attention to detail, and creative vision, the costume designer brings the world of the film to life with authenticity, depth, and visual splendor.

# CHAPTER 4: Life Experience of J. Robert Oppenheimer

J. Robert Oppenheimer, a towering figure in the annals of 20th-century science, led a life marked by brilliance, complexity, and controversy. From his formative years as a precocious intellect to his pivotal role in the development of the atomic bomb and his subsequent fall from grace during the McCarthy era, Oppenheimer's life story is one of triumph and tragedy, genius and moral reckoning.

# Biography of J. Robert Oppenheimer

Born on April 22, 1904, in New York City, J. Robert Oppenheimer was raised in a wealthy, intellectual Jewish family. From a young age, he exhibited extraordinary intellect and curiosity, devouring books on a wide range of subjects and demonstrating a prodigious talent for mathematics and science. After attending the Ethical Culture School and the Alcuin School, Oppenheimer enrolled at Harvard University, where he excelled in physics and earned his bachelor's degree in just three years.

Oppenheimer continued his academic pursuits at the University of Cambridge, where he studied under renowned physicist Patrick Blackett and immersed himself in the vibrant intellectual atmosphere of the

Cavendish Laboratory. It was during this time that Oppenheimer's passion for theoretical physics flourished, laying the groundwork for his groundbreaking contributions to the field.

Upon returning to the United States, Oppenheimer embarked on a distinguished academic career, teaching at institutions such as the University of California, Berkeley, and the California Institute of Technology. His research in quantum mechanics and nuclear physics garnered widespread acclaim, earning him a reputation as one of the brightest minds of his generation.

However, Oppenheimer's life took a dramatic turn with the outbreak of World War II and the onset of the Manhattan Project. Tasked with leading the top-secret effort to develop the atomic bomb, Oppenheimer rose to the occasion, overseeing the construction of the Los Alamos Laboratory and assembling a team of brilliant scientists and engineers.

The successful detonation of the first atomic bomb during the Trinity test in July 1945 marked a turning point in human history, forever altering the course of warfare and geopolitics. Despite his pivotal role in ending World War II, Oppenheimer was haunted by the devastating impact of his creation and the ethical implications of nuclear proliferation.

In the aftermath of the war, Oppenheimer became increasingly vocal about the need for international cooperation and arms control, advocating for civilian control of atomic energy and warning against the dangers of nuclear escalation. However, his outspoken views and association with left-leaning political organizations drew the scrutiny of anti-communist zealots and government officials, leading to his eventual downfall.

In 1954, Oppenheimer's security clearance was revoked following a highly publicized hearing before the Atomic Energy Commission, effectively ending his career as a government advisor and tarnishing his reputation in the eyes of many. Despite this setback, Oppenheimer continued to work as a professor and researcher until his death on February 18, 1967, leaving behind a complex and contested legacy.

# Exploration of Oppenheimer's Personal Struggles, Relationships, and Achievements

Oppenheimer's life was marked by a series of personal struggles, relationships, and achievements that shaped his worldview and legacy. As a young prodigy navigating the competitive world of academia, Oppenheimer grappled with feelings of insecurity and inadequacy, exacerbated by his family's lofty expectations and his own perfectionist tendencies.

Despite his intellectual prowess, Oppenheimer's personal life was often tumultuous and fraught with inner turmoil. His relationships with women, including his wife, Katherine "Kitty" Oppenheimer, and his lover, Jean Tatlock, were characterized by passion, complexity, and, at times, betrayal. Oppenheimer's infidelity and unconventional lifestyle choices strained his marriage and led to periods of emotional upheaval and introspection. Throughout his career, Oppenheimer's achievements in theoretical physics and nuclear research were overshadowed by ethical dilemmas and moral quandaries. As the director of the Manhattan Project, Oppenheimer faced the daunting task of harnessing the power of the atom for the greater good while grappling with the implications of unleashing such destructive force upon the world.

Oppenheimer's advocacy for international cooperation and arms control in the aftermath of World War II reflected his deep-seated commitment to peace and his recognition of the existential threat posed by nuclear weapons. However, his outspoken views and association with leftist political causes made him a target of suspicion and persecution during the McCarthy era, culminating in his public vilification and professional ostracism.

Despite the setbacks and controversies that marred his later years, Oppenheimer's contributions to science and his tireless pursuit of knowledge left an indelible mark on the world. His legacy serves as a cautionary tale about the ethical responsibilities of scientists and the enduring consequences of scientific discovery.

# Comparison of the Film's Depiction of Oppenheimer's Life to Historical Records

"Oppenheimer," the film directed by Christopher Nolan and starring Cillian Murphy, offers a cinematic interpretation of J. Robert Oppenheimer's life that blends historical fact with artistic license. While the film remains faithful to the broad strokes of Oppenheimer's biography, certain aspects of his personal life, relationships, and motivations are inevitably subject to dramatization and narrative embellishment for the sake of storytelling.

For example, the film's portrayal of Oppenheimer's relationships with women, particularly his affair with Jean Tatlock, may take liberties with historical accuracy in order to heighten dramatic tension and character conflict. Similarly, certain pivotal moments in Oppenheimer's career, such as his interactions with military and government officials during the Manhattan Project, may be condensed or simplified for narrative clarity and pacing.

However, despite these artistic liberties, "Oppenheimer" strives to capture the essence of Oppenheimer's character, intellect, and moral dilemmas in a manner that resonates with audiences. Through Cillian Murphy's nuanced performance and Christopher Nolan's masterful direction, the film offers a thought-provoking exploration of Oppenheimer's life and legacy that invites viewers to contemplate the ethical implications of scientific discovery and the enduring complexities of the human condition.

Ultimately, while "Oppenheimer" may not adhere strictly to the historical record, it serves as a compelling portrait of one of the 20th century's most enigmatic figures, shedding light on the man behind the myth and the profound impact of his scientific achievements on the course of history.

# CHAPTER 5: Impact of the Movie

"Oppenheimer," directed by Christopher Nolan and starring Cillian Murphy as the titular character, has made a significant impact on both audiences and the broader cultural landscape since its release. Through its exploration of the life and legacy of J. Robert Oppenheimer and the Manhattan Project, the film has sparked discussions about ethics, scientific responsibility, and the consequences of technological innovation. In this section, we will delve into the cultural significance of "Oppenheimer," its reception among audiences and critics, its influence on perceptions of Oppenheimer and the

Manhattan Project, and its relevance to contemporary issues and concerns.

## Cultural Significance and Reception

"Oppenheimer" premiered at Le Grand Rex in Paris on July 11, 2023, before its theatrical release in the United States and the United Kingdom on July 21. From the outset, the film generated widespread anticipation and excitement, thanks in part to Christopher Nolan's reputation as a visionary filmmaker and the intriguing subject matter of J. Robert Oppenheimer's life.

Upon its release, "Oppenheimer" received acclaim from both audiences and critics alike, who praised its captivating storytelling, stellar performances, and thought-provoking themes. Critics lauded Cillian Murphy's portrayal of Oppenheimer as a nuanced and compelling depiction of a complex historical figure, while also commending Nolan's direction and the film's stunning visual aesthetics.

The film's simultaneous release with Warner Bros.'s "Barbie" led to the emergence of the "Barbenheimer" cultural phenomenon, with audiences encouraged to see both films as a double feature. This unique marketing strategy further heightened the buzz surrounding "Oppenheimer" and contributed to its box office success.

In terms of box office performance, "Oppenheimer" grossed over $959 million worldwide, making it the third-highest-grossing film of 2023 and the highest-grossing biographical film to date. Its commercial success cemented its status as a cultural phenomenon and solidified Nolan's reputation as a box office powerhouse.

## Influence on Audience Perceptions of Oppenheimer and the Manhattan Project

One of the most significant impacts of "Oppenheimer" has been its influence on audience perceptions of J. Robert Oppenheimer and the Manhattan Project. By bringing Oppenheimer's story to the big screen in a compelling and accessible manner, the film has introduced a new generation of viewers to the complexities of his life and the ethical dilemmas he faced.

Through Cillian Murphy's portrayal of Oppenheimer, audiences have gained insight into the inner workings of the brilliant scientist's mind and the moral struggles he grappled with throughout his career. From his leadership of the Manhattan Project to his advocacy for arms control and peace, Oppenheimer emerges as a multifaceted and deeply human figure, challenging preconceived notions and prompting viewers to reconsider their understanding of history.

Similarly, "Oppenheimer" sheds light on the Manhattan Project and its far-reaching consequences, inviting audiences to confront the ethical implications of scientific discovery and technological innovation. By depicting the development and use of the atomic bomb in vivid detail, the film prompts viewers to reflect on the costs of war, the responsibilities of scientists, and the enduring legacy of nuclear weapons in the modern world.

## Discussion of the Film's Relevance to Contemporary Issues and Concerns

"Oppenheimer" resonates with contemporary audiences not only as a historical drama but also as a timely exploration of pressing issues and concerns. In an era marked by geopolitical tensions, technological advancements, and existential threats, the film's themes of scientific responsibility, ethical decision-making, and the quest for peace remain as relevant as ever.

The film's portrayal of Oppenheimer's moral struggle with the consequences of his creations speaks to broader debates surrounding the ethics of scientific research, particularly in fields such as artificial intelligence, genetic engineering, and climate science. As humanity grapples with the implications of emerging technologies and their potential impact on society and the environment, "Oppenheimer" serves as a cautionary tale about the need for ethical oversight and thoughtful consideration of the long-term consequences of scientific innovation. Furthermore, "Oppenheimer" prompts audiences to reflect on the enduring legacy of the Manhattan Project and the ongoing threat posed by nuclear weapons in the 21st century. In an age of nuclear proliferation, arms races, and geopolitical instability, the film's portrayal of Oppenheimer's efforts to promote arms control and disarmament resonates with calls for global cooperation and diplomatic solutions to prevent catastrophic conflict.

In conclusion, "Oppenheimer" has left an indelible mark on audiences and the cultural landscape, sparking discussions about history, ethics, and the human condition. Through its captivating storytelling, compelling performances, and thought-provoking themes, the film has challenged and enlightened viewers, prompting them to reconsider their perceptions of J. Robert Oppenheimer, the Manhattan Project, and the world in which we live.

# CHAPTER 6: Awards and Recognition

"Oppenheimer," directed by Christopher Nolan and featuring Cillian Murphy in the titular role, garnered widespread acclaim upon its release, earning numerous awards and accolades for its stellar performances, captivating storytelling, and technical achievements. In this section, we will explore the awards received by the film, analyze its critical acclaim and industry recognition, and discuss the significance of these accolades for the cast and crew.

# List of Awards Received by the Film

## 1. Academy Awards:

- Best Picture (Nominated)
- Best Director - Christopher Nolan (Nominated)
- Best Actor - Cillian Murphy (Nominated)
- Best Original Screenplay - Christopher Nolan (Nominated)
- Best Cinematography (Won)
- Best Production Design (Won)
- Best Film Editing (Nominated)
- Best Sound Mixing (Nominated)
- Best Original Score (Nominated)

## 2. Golden Globe Awards:

- Best Motion Picture - Drama (Nominated)

- Best Director - Motion Picture (Nominated)
- Best Actor in a Motion Picture - Drama - Cillian Murphy (Nominated)
- Best Original Score - Ludwig Göransson (Nominated)

## 3. BAFTA Awards:

- Best Film (Nominated)
- Best Director - Christopher Nolan (Nominated)
- Best Leading Actor - Cillian Murphy (Nominated)
- Best Original Screenplay - Christopher Nolan (Nominated)
- Best Cinematography (Won)
- Best Production Design (Nominated)
- Best Editing (Nominated)
- Best Sound (Nominated)

- Best Original Music (Nominated)

## 4. Screen Actors Guild Awards:

- Outstanding Performance by a Male Actor in a Leading Role - Cillian Murphy (Nominated)

## 5. Critics' Choice Movie Awards:

- Best Picture (Nominated)
- Best Director - Christopher Nolan (Nominated)
- Best Actor - Cillian Murphy (Nominated)
- Best Original Screenplay - Christopher Nolan (Nominated)
- Best Cinematography (Won)
- Best Production Design (Won)
- Best Editing (Nominated)
- Best Score (Nominated)

## 6. Directors Guild of America Awards:

- Outstanding Directing - Feature Film - Christopher Nolan (Nominated)

## 7. Writers Guild of America Awards:

- Best Original Screenplay - Christopher Nolan (Nominated)

## 8. Producers Guild of America Awards:

- Outstanding Producer of Theatrical Motion Pictures (Nominated)

This list is not exhaustive, as "Oppenheimer" received recognition from numerous other industry organizations and film festivals around the world.

# Analysis of Critical Acclaim and Industry Recognition

"Oppenheimer" received widespread critical acclaim upon its release, with reviewers praising its compelling storytelling, exceptional performances, and stunning visual aesthetics. Christopher Nolan's direction was hailed for its masterful pacing and attention to detail, while Cillian Murphy's portrayal of J. Robert Oppenheimer was lauded as a career-defining performance that captured the complexity and humanity of the enigmatic scientist.

Critics also commended the film's technical achievements, including its cinematography, production design, and sound mixing, which transported audiences to the tumultuous world of the Manhattan Project with immersive realism and authenticity. Ludwig Göransson's haunting score further enhanced the film's emotional impact, complementing Nolan's narrative vision with its evocative melodies and atmospheric soundscapes.

In addition to its critical acclaim, "Oppenheimer" received widespread recognition from industry organizations and awards bodies, earning nominations across multiple categories at prestigious events such as the Academy Awards, Golden Globe Awards, and BAFTA Awards. The film's success at these ceremonies underscored its status as a cinematic achievement of the highest caliber and solidified its place in the pantheon of modern classics.

## Significance of Awards for the Cast and Crew

For the cast and crew of "Oppenheimer," the awards and recognition received by the film represent not only validation of their artistic talent and dedication but also opportunities for career advancement and professional growth. Winning or being nominated for prestigious awards can elevate the profiles of actors, directors, writers, and technicians within the industry, opening doors to new opportunities and collaborations.

For Cillian Murphy, who delivered a career-defining performance as J. Robert Oppenheimer, the accolades received for his portrayal reaffirm his status as one of the most versatile and accomplished actors of his generation. Nominations for Best Actor at the Academy Awards, Golden Globe

Awards, and Screen Actors Guild Awards cement Murphy's reputation as a leading talent in the industry and may lead to future roles in high-profile projects.

Similarly, for Christopher Nolan, whose visionary direction and storytelling prowess have earned him a devoted following among audiences and critics alike, the recognition received for "Oppenheimer" reaffirms his status as one of the most influential filmmakers of his generation. While Nolan has previously been nominated for and won numerous awards for his work, including the Academy Award for Best Original Screenplay for "Inception" (2010), "Oppenheimer" represents another milestone in his illustrious career.

In conclusion, the awards and recognition received by "Oppenheimer" underscore the film's status as a cinematic masterpiece and reaffirm the talent and dedication of its cast and crew. As audiences continue to discover and appreciate the film's profound themes and timeless storytelling, its legacy is sure to endure for years to come, inspiring future generations of filmmakers and audiences alike.

# CHAPTER 7: The Cast and Production

"Oppenheimer," directed by Christopher Nolan and featuring a stellar ensemble cast led by Cillian Murphy, offers a captivating exploration of the life and legacy of J. Robert Oppenheimer and the Manhattan Project. In this section, we will delve into the main cast members and their performances, provide behind-the-scenes insights into the making of the film, and analyze the directorial choices and collaborations that brought the project to life.

# Overview of the Main Cast Members and Their Performances

**1. Cillian Murphy as J. Robert Oppenheimer:** In the titular role, Murphy delivers a tour-de-force performance that captures the complexity and brilliance of the enigmatic scientist. With his piercing gaze and understated intensity, Murphy imbues Oppenheimer with a sense of moral ambiguity and inner turmoil, portraying him as a flawed yet compelling figure grappling with the consequences of his actions.

**2. Emily Blunt as Katherine "Kitty" Oppenheimer:** Blunt shines as Oppenheimer's wife, bringing depth and nuance to her portrayal of a woman caught in the orbit of her husband's towering intellect and turbulent emotions. Blunt's chemistry with Murphy is palpable, conveying the complexities of their relationship with subtlety and sensitivity.

**3. Matt Damon as Gen. Leslie Groves:** Damon delivers a commanding performance as the no-nonsense military leader tasked with overseeing the Manhattan Project. With his steely demeanor and authoritative presence, Damon embodies the military-industrial complex's single-minded pursuit of scientific progress at any cost.

**4. Robert Downey Jr. as Rear Admiral Lewis Strauss:** Downey Jr. brings gravitas and intensity to the role of the government official who spearheads Oppenheimer's downfall. His scenes with Murphy crackle with tension, as their characters clash over matters of national security and personal integrity.

**5. Florence Pugh as Jean Tatlock:** Pugh delivers a haunting performance as Oppenheimer's lover, capturing the troubled spirit of a woman torn between her political ideals and personal demons. Pugh's portrayal adds depth and complexity to the film's exploration of Oppenheimer's personal life and moral dilemmas.

**6. Josh Hartnett as Ernest Lawrence:** Hartnett brings charisma and charm to the role of the pioneering physicist who plays a key role in the development of the atomic bomb. His dynamic interactions with

Murphy's Oppenheimer provide insight into the collaborative nature of scientific discovery.

**7. Casey Affleck as Boris Pash:** Affleck delivers a nuanced performance as the military intelligence officer tasked with investigating Oppenheimer's alleged communist ties. His scenes with Murphy crackle with tension and intrigue, as Pash's relentless pursuit of the truth threatens to unravel Oppenheimer's carefully constructed facade.

**8. Rami Malek as David L. Hill:** Malek brings intelligence and intensity to the role of the brilliant physicist who works alongside Oppenheimer at the Los Alamos Laboratory. His scenes with Murphy showcase the camaraderie and competition that define their relationship as colleagues and friends.

# CHAPTER 8:
# Behind-the-Scenes Insights into the Making of the Film

The production of "Oppenheimer" was a monumental undertaking that required meticulous attention to detail and a collaborative spirit among the cast and crew. From the elaborate sets and period-accurate costumes to the groundbreaking visual effects and evocative score, every aspect of the film was carefully crafted to immerse audiences in the world of the Manhattan Project.

Director Christopher Nolan's visionary approach to filmmaking was evident throughout the production process, as he pushed the boundaries of cinematic storytelling to create a visually stunning and thematically rich portrait of J. Robert Oppenheimer and his era. Nolan's meticulous attention to detail and uncompromising commitment to authenticity ensured that every frame of the film resonated with historical accuracy and emotional depth.

The cast members immersed themselves in their roles, conducting extensive research and drawing inspiration from real-life figures to bring depth and authenticity to their performances. From Cillian Murphy's methodical approach to embodying Oppenheimer's intellect and inner turmoil to Emily Blunt's nuanced portrayal of Kitty Oppenheimer's resilience and vulnerability, each actor brought their character to life with precision and passion.

The production team also faced numerous challenges along the way, from recreating the top-secret laboratories of the Manhattan Project to capturing the complex interpersonal dynamics that defined Oppenheimer's world. Through meticulous planning, innovative techniques, and a relentless pursuit of excellence, the cast and crew overcame these obstacles to create a cinematic experience that resonated with audiences around the world.

## Directorial Choices and Collaborations

Christopher Nolan's directorial choices and collaborations were instrumental in shaping the artistic vision of "Oppenheimer" and bringing the project to fruition. Known for his bold storytelling and innovative filmmaking techniques, Nolan approached the material with a keen eye for detail and a deep reverence for the subject matter.

Nolan's decision to tell Oppenheimer's story in a nonlinear fashion, weaving together past and present events to create a multi-layered narrative, added complexity and depth to the film's exploration of the scientist's life and legacy. By juxtaposing moments of triumph and tragedy, Nolan invited audiences to contemplate the ethical implications of Oppenheimer's actions and the enduring consequences of his scientific discoveries.

Collaborating closely with cinematographer Hoyte van Hoytema, Nolan crafted a visually stunning and thematically rich cinematic experience that transported audiences to the turbulent world of the Manhattan Project. Through innovative camera techniques, immersive sound design, and breathtaking visual effects, Nolan and his team brought Oppenheimer's story to life with unparalleled cinematic spectacle.

In addition to his collaborations with the technical team, Nolan worked closely with the cast to develop their characters and bring authenticity to their performances. Through open communication, creative exploration, and mutual respect, Nolan fostered an environment of collaboration and experimentation that empowered the actors to fully inhabit their roles and deliver standout performances.

In conclusion, "Oppenheimer" stands as a testament to the power of collaborative storytelling and the transformative potential of cinema. Through the dedication and talent of its cast and crew, the film offers a poignant and thought-provoking exploration of one of the most pivotal moments in human history, inviting audiences to grapple with the complexities of science, morality, and the human condition.

# CHAPTER 9: Additional Information

"Oppenheimer," directed by Christopher Nolan and featuring Cillian Murphy in the lead role, has left a lasting impact on audiences worldwide. In addition to its compelling storytelling and stellar performances, the film has sparked numerous trivia, comparisons to other biographical films or historical dramas, and fan reactions and theories. In this section, we will explore these aspects of "Oppenheimer" and delve into the additional information surrounding the film.

# Trivia about the Film

**1. Historical Accuracy:** Despite being a work of fiction, "Oppenheimer" strives for historical accuracy in its portrayal of J. Robert Oppenheimer and the Manhattan Project. Christopher Nolan and his team conducted extensive research to ensure that the film's depiction of events and characters remained faithful to the historical record.

**2. Locations:** The film was shot on location in various places, including the University of California, Berkeley, the California Institute of Technology, and the Los Alamos Laboratory. These authentic settings helped to immerse the cast and crew in the world of the Manhattan Project and bring Oppenheimer's story to life with authenticity.

**3. Costumes and Wardrobe:** The film's costume designer meticulously recreated the fashions of the 1930s and 1940s, drawing inspiration from historical photographs and documents. From Oppenheimer's tailored suits to Kitty Oppenheimer's elegant dresses, every costume was designed to reflect the period and enhance the character's authenticity.

**4. Sound Design:** The film's immersive sound design played a crucial role in creating the atmosphere and mood of the Manhattan Project. From the rumble of explosions to the hum of scientific equipment, every sound was carefully crafted to transport audiences to the world of Los Alamos and evoke the tension and excitement of the era.

**5. Cameo Appearances:** Christopher Nolan is known for making cameo appearances in his own films, and "Oppenheimer" is no exception. Eagle-eyed viewers may spot Nolan in a brief cameo role, adding an extra layer of intrigue to the film's behind-the-scenes trivia.

## Comparison to Other Biographical Films or Historical Dramas

**1. "The Imitation Game" (2014):** Like "Oppenheimer," "The Imitation Game" explores the life of a brilliant scientist – in this case, mathematician Alan Turing – and his contributions to a pivotal moment in history – the breaking of the Enigma code during World War II. Both films grapple with themes of genius, secrecy, and sacrifice, offering audiences a glimpse into the lives of extraordinary individuals who changed the course of history.

**2. "Schindler's List" (1993):** While "Schindler's List" focuses on a different aspect of World War II – the Holocaust and the efforts of Oskar Schindler to save Jewish lives – it shares thematic similarities with "Oppenheimer." Both films explore the moral complexities of war and the human capacity for both good and evil, challenging audiences to confront difficult questions about responsibility, complicity, and redemption.

**3. "The Theory of Everything" (2014):**
Like "Oppenheimer," "The Theory of Everything" is a biographical drama that delves into the personal and professional life of a renowned scientist – in this case, physicist Stephen Hawking. Both films offer intimate portraits of their subjects, exploring the triumphs and tragedies that shaped their lives and careers, while also shedding light on the broader social and historical context in which they lived.

## Fan Reactions and Theories

**1. Praise for Cillian Murphy:** Fans and critics alike have praised Cillian Murphy's performance as J. Robert Oppenheimer, hailing it as one of the actor's most compelling and nuanced roles to date. Murphy's ability to convey the scientist's inner turmoil and moral ambiguity has earned him widespread acclaim and cemented his status as a leading talent in the industry.

**2. Debate Over Historical Accuracy:** While "Oppenheimer" strives for historical accuracy, some viewers have questioned certain aspects of the film's portrayal of events and characters. From minor discrepancies in dialogue to broader interpretations of Oppenheimer's motivations and actions, fans have engaged in lively debates about the film's fidelity to the historical record.

**3.     Exploration     of     Themes:** "Oppenheimer" explores a wide range of themes, including the ethics of scientific research, the consequences of technological innovation, and the moral dilemmas faced by individuals caught in the midst of war. Fans have dissected these themes in detail, drawing connections to contemporary issues and engaging in thoughtful discussions about the film's broader implications.

In conclusion, "Oppenheimer" has sparked numerous trivia, comparisons, and fan reactions since its release, reflecting its impact on audiences and the broader cultural conversation. From its meticulous attention to historical detail to its exploration of timeless themes and complex characters, the film continues to captivate viewers and inspire discussions long after the credits have rolled.

# CONCLUSION

In this comprehensive guide, we have delved deep into the world of "Oppenheimer," exploring its plot, characters, production, impact, and more. As we conclude our journey through this captivating film, let's summarize the key takeaways from our exploration and reflect on its enduring legacy and impact.

## Summary of Key Takeaways from the Guide

Throughout this guide, we have uncovered the intricate layers of "Oppenheimer," beginning with an overview of the film's plot, characters, and historical context. From J. Robert Oppenheimer's tumultuous personal life to his pivotal role in the development of the atomic bomb, the film offers a gripping exploration of one of the most consequential moments in human history. We then delved into the film's production, analyzing its meticulous attention to detail, stunning visuals, and standout performances. From Cillian Murphy's riveting portrayal of Oppenheimer to Christopher Nolan's visionary direction, every aspect of the film was crafted with precision and passion, resulting in a cinematic experience that resonated with audiences worldwide.

As we explored the impact of "Oppenheimer," we discovered its cultural significance and reception, its influence on audience perceptions of Oppenheimer and the Manhattan Project, and its relevance to contemporary issues and concerns. From critical acclaim and industry recognition to fan reactions and theories, the film sparked discussions and debates that continue to resonate long after its release.

## Final Thoughts on the Film's Legacy and Enduring Impact

"Oppenheimer" stands as a towering achievement in cinematic storytelling, offering a thought-provoking exploration of science, morality, and the human condition. By weaving together historical events with intimate character portraits, the film invites audiences to grapple with the complexities of war, power, and responsibility, challenging us to confront difficult questions about the nature of progress and the price of innovation. As we reflect on the film's legacy, we are reminded of the enduring power of storytelling to illuminate the past, inspire the present, and shape the future. "Oppenheimer" serves as a testament to the resilience of the human spirit and the importance of reckoning with our collective history, reminding us of the ethical implications of our actions and the consequences of our choices.

In the years to come, "Oppenheimer" will continue to captivate and inspire audiences, sparking conversations and debates about the nature of science, the ethics of warfare, and the fragility of the human condition. Through its compelling narrative, powerful performances, and thought-provoking themes, the film leaves an indelible mark on the cinematic landscape, ensuring its place among the great works of art that challenge, provoke, and illuminate our understanding of the world.

In conclusion, "Oppenheimer" is more than just a film – it is a profound meditation on the complexities of the human experience and a poignant reminder of the enduring power of the human spirit to triumph over adversity. As we bid farewell to this cinematic masterpiece, we carry with us its lessons, its insights, and its enduring legacy, forever enriched by the journey it has taken us on.

www.ingramcontent.com/pod-product-compliance
Lightning Source LLC
Chambersburg PA
CBHW050834260726
48660CB00006B/2244